POLICE DOGS

Rosie Albright

PowerKiDS
press™

New York

Published in 2012 by The Rosen Publishing Group, Inc.
29 East 21st Street, New York, NY 10010

First Edition

Editor: Joanne Randolph
Book Design: Kate Laczynski

Photo Credits: Cover Jay Town/Newspix/Getty Images; pp. 5, 24 (right) Matt Cardy/Getty Images; p. 6 Matt King/Getty Images; pp. 8–9, 18, 20–21, 24 (left, center) Shutterstock.com; p. 10 Billy Hustace/Getty Images; p. 13 Justin Sullivan/Getty Images; pp. 14–15 Nicholas Kamm/ AFP/Getty Images; p. 17 Jim Frazee/Getty Images; p. 23 Mike Albans/NY Daily News Archive via Getty Images.

Library of Congress Cataloging-in-Publication Data

Albright, Rosie.
 Police dogs / by Rosie Albright. — 1st ed.
    p. cm. — (Animal detectives)
 Includes index.
 ISBN 978-1-4488-6148-4 (library binding) — ISBN 978-1-4488-6254-2 (pbk.) —
 ISBN 978-1-4488-6255-9 (6-pack)
 1. Police dogs—Juvenile literature. I. Title.
 HV8025.A434 2012
 363.2'32—dc23

                                        2011020672

Manufactured in the United States of America

CPSIA Compliance Information: Batch #WW12PK: For Further Information contact Rosen Publishing, New York, New York at 1-800-237-9932

CONTENTS

Police Dogs   4

A Big Job   8

In Training   19

Words to Know   24

Index   24

Web Sites   24

Police dogs do important jobs. They work to keep people safe.

Police dogs work with a **handler**. An officer and dog are called a K-9 team.

The most common
kind of police dog is
the German shepherd.

Police dogs look for illegal things. They sniff out drugs and **bombs**.

Police dogs use their noses to track people and search buildings.

14

Dogs smell so well that they can smell a person who is under **rubble**. They can smell things buried underground, too.

Police dogs often wear special vests. The vests show they are working.

SEARCH DOG

17

The first K-9 units were trained in Belgium. One of the first American K-9 units was formed in Baltimore, Maryland.

Today many K-9 units train their dogs the same way Baltimore does. Running an **obstacle course** is one part of training.

Police dogs are animal detectives. They are ready to help whenever they are needed.

WORDS TO KNOW

bomb

obstacle course

handler

rubble

INDEX

B
bombs, 11

H
handler, 7

P
people, 4,
    12, 15

V
vests, 16

WEB SITES

Due to the changing nature of Internet links, PowerKids Press has developed an online list of Web sites related to the subject of this book. This site is updated regularly. Please use this link to access the list:
www.powerkidslinks.com/andt/dogs/

24